TALYLLYN RAILWAY
A JOURNEY BY STEAM

by James Waite

DOLGOCH and TALYLLYN head up the valley above Tan-y-coed Uchaf on 31st March 2017.

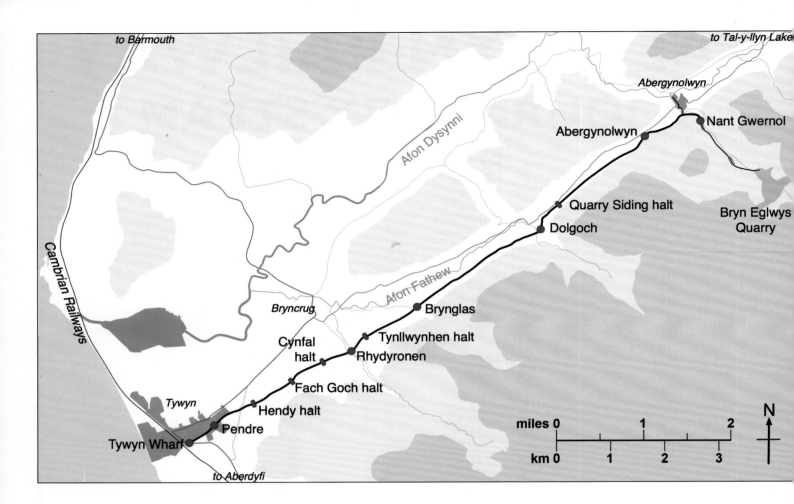

Published by Mainline & Maritime Ltd, 3 Broadleaze, Upper Seagry, near Chippenham, SN15 5EY
Tel: 01275 845012
www.mainlineandmaritime.co.uk   orders@mainlineandmaritime.co.uk
Printed in the UK

ISBN: 978-1-900340-66-3   © Mainline & Maritime Ltd, & Author 2020
All photographs by the Author
Cover images are reproduced and captioned in the text
Map above from Wikimedia

INTRODUCTION

Welcome to this photo album of the Talyllyn Railway. The TR has an impressive list of attributes – the first narrow gauge railway anywhere in the world to have been designed and built for operation as a steam-powered passenger line and the first to have been taken over by enthusiasts, back in 1950 when closure seemed inevitable. Its rescue paved the way for the worldwide preservation movement we know today. It is also one of only two nineteenth century railways which still operate all their original locomotives and coaches – the other being the little Chiemseebahn in Bavaria.

The Talyllyn has always been a personal favourite of mine amongst the Welsh narrow gauge lines. Even though it now carries many more passengers than it ever saw in the days before preservation it has always retained the character of a small rural railway, with short trains hauled by little engines, calling at tiny stations which look little different now than they did more than a century ago. Most of all it serves a delightful district which has always been slightly off the beaten track and is operated by people who clearly enjoy what they do. They unfailingly provide a warm welcome to their visitors, be they families on a day out or enthusiasts asking for access to areas which would be off-limits on many other railways.

For all heritage railways in the UK and right across the northern hemisphere the Covid-19 outbreak could not have come at a more difficult time and the Talyllyn is no exception. Bills for things like staff costs accrue all year round. Most of the income to pay them comes from ticket sales in the spring and summer but this year the trains are not running. Easter came in the middle of a period of glorious sunshine which would normally have seen large numbers of tourists visiting Mid-Wales and travelling on the Talyllyn's trains. Instead it has been the first Easter since 1953 when the trains have been at a standstill. Like everyone else the railway's volunteers are locked down at home. As I write this nearly all the paid staff have been furloughed, the locos and coaches are locked away and weeds grow along rusty rails – and there is no clear indication of when things will change.

I'm most grateful to Lawrence Garvey, Keith Theobald, Will Smith, John Smallwood, Don Marshall and Peter Stowell for their help and for answering my requests for information extremely quickly, in line with the tight timetable called for in preparing this little book. The railway has launched an appeal for funds to help it through this difficult time and I am delighted to be have been able to produce the book, the profits from which will all go towards the appeal. I hope that the photos will, in a modest way, provide a little of the pleasure that, in happier times, would have come from a journey through the mountains from the seaside at Tywyn. They all date from the last fifteen years and I have laid them out to present a virtual version of that journey. Sit back and enjoy the ride!

James Waite

The end of the line, or should that be the beginning?! 0-4-2ST no 3 SIR HAYDN (Hughes 323/1878) stands at the buffer stop at Tywyn Wharf station and whistles before running round her train on 22 August 2005. The name commemorates Sir Henry Haydn Jones, the district's MP. In 1911 he bought the line and the Bryn Eglwys slate quarry which it served. They were already unprofitable, and his objective seems mainly to have been to preserve the jobs which the quarry provided. It became unsafe and was closed in 1947, but he kept the railway running until he died in 1950. The whistle now fitted to SIR HAYDN was originally a spare for the British Railways Britannia class Pacifics working out of Stratford shed in east London on the Great Eastern mainline.

Jeff Shuttleworth is driving as SIR HAYDN runs round her train at Wharf. She is one of two Talyllyn locos which spent their working lives on the Corris Railway, only a few miles away, and was running in an accurate reproduction of her old Corris Indian red livery. The large station building at Wharf was completed a few months before I took this photo on 17 May 2005. Most of it is occupied by the Narrow Gauge Railway Museum and by the railway's café.

A view at Wharf over a small flowerbed towards SIR HAYDN as she waits to set off with an afternoon train on 13 April 2007. The Corris Railway was a part of the Great Western in its later years and duly became a part of British Railways on 1 January 1948. It closed only seven months later. The late Campbell Thomas, the stationmaster at Machynlleth who had charge of the line, knew that its two locos could be valuable additions to the Talyllyn's stock and liked to keep them sheeted over, and hidden behind a line of standard gauge wagons, so that they would be away from the prying eyes of higher authority.

SIR HAYDN at Wharf, again on 13 April 2007. One of the preservation society's first acts in 1951 was to send representatives to Swindon works to negotiate the purchase of one of the two Corris locos. The asking price was said to be £65 each, but after pleading the Talyllyn's case they were offered the two for £50, reputedly their written-down value in the GWR's last accounts.

Mark Freeman, Kathryn Smith and John Robinson are coaling 0-4-0T no 2 DOLGOCH (Fletcher Jennings 63/1866) at Wharf in a view seen from the museum balcony on 22 August 2005. The van to the right, no 146, is the only survivor of three or four which ran on the old railway. After it was withdrawn in 1932 its body was moved to Rhydyronen and used as a garden shed by Hugh Jones, a long-standing staff member, who lived in a cottage there provided by Sir Haydn. *Llechfan*, the bungalow to the left in this photo, is used as a hostel for volunteers.

DOLGOCH waits at Wharf to take the first train of the day up the valley on 22 August 2005. Part of the building to the left is the original pre-1950 structure. It now houses the railway shop and offices. DOLGOCH was the railway's only working loco in 1950, though "working" was a relative term and, like most things at the railway, the loco was completely worn out. Sir Haydn had sent her to the Atlas Foundry in Shrewsbury for repair in 1945 and she returned carrying this attractive light green livery. She carried t again for a few years in the early 2000s.

For once DOLGOCH is not the focus of everyone's attention as British Railways 2-6-0 no 76079 (Horwich, 1957) passes Wharf with a steam special from Machynlleth to Barmouth on 22 August 2005. Summer steam services on the Cambrian Coast Railway were popular during the early 2000s but new signalling arrangements have brought them to an end. Economy was the order of the day in the pre-preservation era. All the station platforms have always been on the northern side of the line so there was no need to paint the names of the railway and the loco on the southern one!

0-4-2T no 7 TOM ROLT arrives at Wharf on 22 August 2005. The loco was rebuilt over many years at the Talyllyn's Pendre works from a 3ft gauge 0-4-0T, one of three built for Bord na Móna, the Irish state peat authority, as their no 1 (Andrew Barclay 2269/1949).

TOM ROLT runs round her train at Wharf on 22 August 2005. She was named after the preservation society's principal founder.

On 9 July 2014 DOLGOCH sets off from Wharf. She's painted in what was believed to have been her paint scheme in the early years of the twentieth century. The leading coach was originally Corris Railway no 8 and GWR no 4992. All the Corris coaches were withdrawn when passenger services on the line ended in 1931 and moved for storage to Oswestry works. No 4992, and one other coach, were later sold to a GWR staff member and taken to the garden at his home at Gobowen. It was acquired by the Talyllyn in 1958, extensively rebuilt and re-entered service in 1961.

0-4-2ST no 4 EDWARD THOMAS (Kerr Stuart 4047/1921) was the other Corris loco bought in 1951. Here she takes water at Wharf on 1 April 2017.

EDWARD THOMAS runs round her train at Wharf on 1 April 2017. She is named after Sir Haydn's long-serving manager. After Sir Haydn's death his estate passed to his widow. She generously passed the railway to the preservation society and it is believed that Edward Thomas's encouragement, and advice that the preservationists knew what they were doing, played a key role in her decision. He continued to serve the railway and his knowledge and experience were invaluable.

EDWARD THOMAS has whistled for her departure and her drain cocks are open as she sets off from Wharf on 1 April 2017. Very appropriately for an ex-GWR loco in preservation she was fitted with her the larger of the two whistles carried by no 7007 GREAT WESTERN, the last Castle class 4-6-0 to be built at Swindon for the old railway before it was nationalised. The smaller one was fitted to TALYLLYN. They were a gift from the late Roy Smith, a long-term Talyllyn driver. He had to go to enormous lengths to rescue them since it turned out that the loco had already been sold to scrap merchants, although she was still at Worcester engine shed, always a popular place with enthusiasts since its spectacular location at the bottom of a cliff made for excellent photography, and the staff were unfailingly welcoming. It was also the base for the locos working the last regular express trains anywhere on the old GWR system. Once the problem had been explained to Roy he tracked down the scrapmen's office, negotiated their purchase, paid for them and then returned to Worcester with his receipt to claim them.

0-4-2ST no 1 TALYLLYN (Fletcher Jennings 42/1864) was the railway's first loco. She was built as a 0-4-0ST but the long overhang at the back caused trouble and, soon after DOLGOCH arrived in 1866, she returned to her builders to have a rear axle fitted. Here she stands at Wharf with the original coaches on the evening of 9 August 2015. It was a gala weekend, and the train was waiting to take customers at the railway's beer festival for a late night journey up the valley.

DOLGOCH, on the left, and TALYLLYN, on the right, stand at Wharf for a photographic event on the evening of 22 March 2016 with two slate wagons. The two locos were restored to what is believed to be their original livery during the winter of 2014-5. Much of the credit for this goes to Martin Fuller, a long-term Talyllyn driver, who has carried out a vast amount of research and whose 3-volume history of the Talyllyn and Corris locos is likely to remain the definitive work on the subject for many years to come. *Trefri*, the mock-Tudor house in the background, was for many years Edward Thomas's home and was purchased for the railway in 2019.

DOLGOCH and TALYLLYN stand at Wharf on 20 March 2018. The wagon with the GW lettering is one of several which followed the two Corris locos from Machynlleth to Tywyn in 1951.

TALYLLYN arrives at Wharf on 19 March 2018. In 1945 she ran for the last time before preservation, probably on an occasion when DOLGOCH had derailed and required rescue. In 1957 she left Pendre for rebuilding in the Midlands and first steamed again in the following year.

DOLGOCH takes water at Wharf on 5 July 2019. The cast iron lamp is one supplied as part of a gas lighting scheme for Porthmadog in 1857 by the De Winton foundry at Caernarfon, best known for its vertical-boilered locos which it supplied to many North Wales slate quarries in the nineteenth century.

The lettering on the De Winton lamp standard. 5 July 2019.

Andrew Thomas, the driver of 0-4-0T no 6 DOUGLAS (Andrew Barclay 1431/1918), attends to her motion at Wharf before setting off up the valley on 11 March 2014. The loco was built for the Air Service Constructional Corps in 1918. She had been temporarily repainted in her original livery, complete with the handsome brass replica plate in this photo. DOUGLAS and the Irish peat loco in her original form were members of their builders' E class, though both were modified to suit their purchasers' requirements. After service at RAF Manston in Kent she moved in 1921 to the RAF's 2ft gauge railway at Calshot in Hampshire where she worked until 1945.

The Narrow Gauge Railway Museum at Tywyn dates from the preservation society's early years and has a splendid collection of exhibits from all over the British Isles. Dundee Gasworks' 1ft 11½ ins or 597mm gauge 0-4-0WT no 2 (Kerr Stuart 720/1907) became an exhibit in 1961. She was extensively restored in 2004 and looked pristine when I saw her on 22 August 2005. In July 2017 she moved on long-term loan to Beamish museum in County Durham.

The Dorking Greystone Lime Company's 3ft 2¼ ins or 972mm gauge 0-4-0T WILLIAM FINLAY (Fletcher Jennings 173L/1880) was bought for the museum in 2015 and was one of two similar locos which spent their working lives at Betchworth Quarry in the North Downs. The other, TOWNSEND HOOK, is now at Amberley Museum in West Sussex. The quarry was also home to a standard gauge Fletcher Jennings 0-4-0T, CAPTAIN BAXTER, which now runs on the Bluebell Railway in East Sussex. They both visited the Talyllyn in 2016; this get-together for the five UK Fletcher Jennings locos amongst the world's nine survivors was a definite first! WILLIAM FINLAY had just been installed in the museum when I visited on 1st April 2017 and her name- and works-plates had yet to be fitted. Behind her is a 2ft gauge 4wPM (Baguley 774/1919) which has also been an exhibit since 2017. She was built for a government forest tramway at Pennal, over the hill to the south of Abergynolwyn, and later worked at the Oakeley slate quarries at Blaenau Ffestiniog.

The 1ft 10¾ ins or 578mm gauge 0-4-0 VBT GEORGE HENRY was built by De Winton in 1877 for the huge Penrhyn slate quarry at Bethesda. She was a beefed up version of the normal De Winton design and I took this overhead view on 5 July 2019 to emphasise her larger boiler. She spent her entire working life at Penrhyn and was donated to the museum in 1964.

0-4-0ST ROUGH PUP (Hunslet 541/1891) is one of eleven Alice class locos built between 1886 and 1904 for the Dinorwic slate quarries at Llanberis, all of which have been preserved. The railways there were also 1ft 10¾ ins or 578mm gauge. ROUGH PUP was donated to the museum in 1968, and is the only one of the eleven which is still in her original Dinorwic condition in all respects. 5 July 2019.

The long and narrow Giesl ejector, a novel form of exhaust system and chimney invented by an Austrian engineer, was claimed to improve the fuel efficiency of a steam loco by between 6% and 12%. Its inventor offered one to British Railways free of charge for test purposes but was rebuffed. He then made the offer to the Talyllyn which fitted the ejector to EDWARD THOMAS in 1958. Initial tests suggested an improvement of up to 40% but after the device wore out and was replaced by a conventional chimney in 1969 the loco's performance remained much the same. The ejector is now an exhibit at the museum. 5 July 2019.

TALYLLYN and DOLGOCH stand inside the engine shed at Tywyn Pendre on 20 March 2016. The shed dates back to the railway's earliest years.

Chris Parry, the gentleman on the left and then the railway's general manager, casts a watchful eye over the motion of DOLGOCH as she raises steam at Pendre on 9 July 2014.

Ross Waddington and Paul Edwards, two volunteers, attend to EDWARD THOMAS at Pendre before her day's work on 5 July 2018.

With four locos in residence on the evening of 12 April 2007 Pendre shed is full! Until the loco stock expanded in preservation the part occupied by TOM ROLT and SIR HAYDN, the two locos nearest the camera, was a cottage provided for a staff member – an extreme case of living on the job! The original shed was the section nearest the door occupied by DOLGOCH, in green, and DOUGLAS, in red, all that was needed when the railway only owned two locos.

Next to the loco shed is the site of the original carriage shed, now an appendage to the loco shed and works, where TALYLLYN and EDWARD THOMAS stood on 12 April 2007. TALYLLYN was supplied by her builders without a cab, though the vagaries of the Welsh weather led to one being fitted by 1866. Here the cab had been removed temporarily to recreate her original appearance.

Loco repairs are still carried out in the workshop which was built at Pendre in the railway's very early years. By 21st century standards it's a very cramped working environment. Plans have been prepared to relocate to a modern unit but with the onset of the Covid-19 pandemic all major projects have been put on hold. TOM ROLT was under repair on 10 March 2014.

The Talyllyn possesses nine bogie coaches which are relatively modern, albeit of traditional appearance. They are essential for maintaining the railway's summer services when three train sets are in operation. The prototype, no 18, was built as a volunteer project between 1961 and 1965, and was undergoing major refurbishment in the carriage shop, a part of the south carriage shed at Pendre, on 10 March 2014.

The wheel lathe, complete with a carriage wheelset, on 10 March 2014.

On 9 July 2014 DOLGOCH draws a train out of the north carriage shed at Pendre. The leading vehicle is the original passenger brake van no 5. It was built by Brown Marshalls of Birmingham in 1865, one year before then the first passenger coach. This is its southern, non-platform, side on which there is only a minimal need for doors.

At Pendre DOLGOCH stands at the head of a train consisting of all the historic coaches on 5 July 2018. She is preparing to propel them down to Wharf to work the Victorian Train service, which in recent years has operated every Thursday in June, July and September. It involves a 5-hour guided round trip including runpasts and a lunch break at Abergynolwyn.

DOLGOCH stands outside the old carriage shed in the evening of 9 July 2014. Despite being almost worn-out she worked all the preservation society's trains during its first year and much of the second until the Corris locos could take over. She was overhauled in the Midlands between 1954 and 1963.

TOM ROLT shunts DOLGOCH into the engine shed in the evening of 9 July 2014.

On the evening of 20 March 2016 DOLGOCH and TALYLLYN show off their attractive historic paint schemes outside the old carriage shed.

On 6 July 2017 TOM ROLT heads the first train on the day away from Pendre, and approaches Ty Mawr bridge, about half a mile further up the line.

DOLGOCH catches a brief glimpse of sunshine as she passes Hendy farm with a mixed train, including some slate wagons at its rear, during a gala on 9 August 2015.

DOLGOCH approaches Ty Mawr bridge on 9 August 2015 with the same train.

DOUGLAS passes Ty Mawr bridge as she heads up the line with an engineering train on 10 March 2014. The Calshot line possessed two of these Barclay locos, and in 1949 they were bought at auction by Abelson & Co (Engineers) Ltd of Birmingham, probably as a speculative venture as they hoped to resell them for service in India. This failed as the locos' mudhole doors didn't match up to Indian regulations. DOUGLAS was donated to the Talyllyn in 1953, and is named after Douglas Abelson who was responsible for passing her to them.

Cheery waves all round as TALYLLYN passes Hendy bridge on 6 July 2017. They weren't for me but for my 11-month old granddaughter!

Hendy bridge is an unusual structure. It carries a public bridleway over the line at an oblique angle which then turns sharply to run beside the line, requiring the retaining wall to the left of this photo. DOLGOCH approaches with a down train on 4 July 2019.

On 2 July 2017 TALYLLYN approaches Hendy bridge with a down train.

DOUGLAS heads up the valley between Hendy and Fach Goch on 5 July 2017.

TOM ROLT between Fach Goch and Hendy with a down train on 3 July 2017. The bridleway which begins at Hendy runs close to the railway as a public right of way all the way up the valley as far as Brynglas. There are some excellent walks, which can be combined with a ride on the train to any of the stations and halts on this part of the line.

TOM ROLT passes Cynfal Halt with the last down train of the day on 6 July 2018.

DOUGLAS heads through Rhydyronen station, with its splendid display of daffodils, in the hazy early morning sunshine on 11 March 2014.

The same location looks very different in high summer! DOLGOCH draws to a halt at Rhydyronen on 9 July 2014.

Gareth Jones has charge of DOLGOCH as the Victorian Train arrives at Rhdyronen on 5 July 2018. Gareth first volunteered at the Talyllyn more than fifty years ago.

DOLGOCH poses for photographs at Rhydyronen on 31 March 2017. The bridges here and at Ty Mawr were built a few years later than the others and at a time when supplies of slate from Bryn Eglwys quarry had become readily available. In contrast to Hendy and the other original bridges the roadway is supported by slate slabs resting on girders, no doubt more economical to build than an arched bridge.

Gareth Jones and fireman Matthew Shield take DOLGOCH away from Rhydyronen bridge on 5 July 2018. The body of covered van no 146 used to stand next to the bridge, and the bank to the right of this photo was once the site of Hugh Jones's garden.

TALYLLYN and DOLGOCH head up the valley near Tynllwyn Hen with a mixed train on 20 March 2018. This was part of a series of photo-charters which have been arranged annually on behalf of the railway for many years by David Williams, an experienced operator in this field.

Another view of the same train near Tynllwyn Hen on 20 March 2018.

Geufron farm on the far side of the Fathew valley, and the mobile home holiday park alongside it, form the backdrop to this photo on 20 March 2018. The "beast from the east" blizzard had struck much of the UK two days previously. The Tywyn district seldom sees snowfall and was only lightly affected, but there are traces in the foreground of this photo.

The daffodils are in full bloom on 11 March 2014 as DOUGLAS arrives at Brynglas loop with what looks like a ballast train, but was in reality arranged for another of Mr Williams's photo charters.

More daffodils at Brynglas on 20 March 2018. DOLGOCH approaches as TALYLLYN stands in the loop.

DOLGOCH approaches Brynglas station as TALYLLYN stands in the loop on 20 March 2018.

DOLGOCH passes Brynglas block post, as the Talyllyn calls its signal boxes, on 20 March 2018.

TALYLLYN enters Brynglas station on 20 March 2018. Note the slate fencing in the foreground, very characteristic of the Welsh slate-mining districts. The loco was in the last weeks of her 10-year boiler certificate and was withdrawn in June 2018. Her overhaul at Pendre was well-advanced by March 2020 but then became a victim of the Covid-19 suspension of major work. At present it is unclear when it will restart.

TOM ROLT approaches Brynglas station with a down train on the evening of 9 July 2014.

Fireman Chris Parrott looks ahead down the line as DOLGOCH waits for time at Brynglas with the last down train of the day on 14 October 2005. For many years Chris has shared his railway activities between the Talyllyn in the northern summer and the 500mm gauge Ferrocarril Austral Fueguino at Ushuaia, on Tierra del Fuego at the southernmost tip of Argentina, in the southern one.

DOLGOCH catches the late the autumnal evening sunshine at Brynglas on the same occasion. The Ushuaia line markets itself as *El Tren del Fin del Mundo*, or *The Train at the End of the World*. It was built as a 600mm gauge line in the early 1900s to serve a penal colony. Chris is the author of a book about its history. The content is so thorough and well-researched that there's little that anyone else could possibly add!

TALYLLYN and DOLGOCH arrive at Brynglas on the evening of 19 March 2018.

DOUGLAS heads up the valley east of Brynglas on 12 March 2014.

DOUGLAS heads towards the woods east of Brynglas on 12 March 2014. The small 4-wheeled vehicle nearest the camera i[s] Corris Railway van no 11, supplied by the Falcon works at Loughborough in 1885. It accompanied nearly all Corris trains unt[il] the line closed in 1948 and was latterly GWR no 8754. It must have been downgraded from its passenger status during the GWR era as it arrived at Tywyn in 1951 painted in their freight wagon grey.

's almost sunset as DOUGLAS approaches the woods between Brynglas and Dolgoch on 12 March 2014.

A silhouette view of DOUGLAS east of Brynglas at sunset on 12 March 2014.

The going-away shot of the same train on 12 March 2014.

Another sunset photo at the same location, this time of TALYLLYN and DOLGOCH on 19 March 2018.

TALYLLYN and DOLGOCH with the same train on 19 March 2018, a little nearer Dolgoch, with the last of the snow as a backdrop.

TALYLLYN and DOLGOCH approach the woods east of Brynglas with the same train, on 19 March 2018.

TALYLLYN at sunset on 19 March 2018.

The setting sun glints off the train east of Brynglas on 19 March 2018.

The same location the following morning as DOLGOCH and TALYLLYN work a mixed train up the valley. This is one of the finest photo spots anywhere on the railway but it's worth mentioning that there is no public right of way and the charters which Mr Williams organises provide the only opportunities for access. Dolau Gwyn, a magnificent seventeenth century manor house, can be seen to the right on the far side of the valley. Unfortunately it is not usually open to the public.

The going-away shot of the same train on 19 March 2018, the tree being the one beneath which I had photographed TALYLLYN at sunset the previous evening.

Further to the east DOLGOCH and TALYLLYN head up the valley on 20 March 2018.

DOLGOCH and TALYLLYN, at a place known amongst the railway's staff as Six Bends. Dol-Deheuwydd farm stands on the valley road, and in the distance the sun lights up snow on the slopes of Cadair Idris, the third-highest mountain in Wales. 20 March 2018.

The railway runs through woods on the approach to Dolgoch and, without warning save for a brief whistle, the train emerges to cross Dolgoch viaduct, the most substantial engineering structure on the railway. Here's SIR HAYDN on 13 April 2007. She has carried the same number under the Corris, the GWR, British Railways and the Talyllyn. EDWARD THOMAS has only carried the same number after becoming a GWR loco and she appears never to have been numbered on the Corris.

This is another scene which looks quite different in high summer. Most of the viaduct is lost amongst the trees as DOLGOCH crosses it with the Victorian Train on 4 July 2019. The lowest of the three Dolgoch waterfalls is only about 100 metres to the south. It's just out of sight from the train but can clearly be heard on a still day.

DOLGOCH crosses the viaduct on 9 July 2014, seen from the footpath leading from the station to the falls.

Just over one year later DOLGOCH wears her original Indian Red colour while working a train during the gala on 9 August 2015.

TALYLLYN crosses the viaduct on 6 July 2017 with the Victorian Train.

This is one of the places where the Victorian Train makes a runpast, which gave an opportunity for a second photo of TALYLLYN on 6 July 2017.

DOLGOCH and TALYLLYN stand at Dolgoch station on 21 March 2016 during another of Mr Williams's photo charters. Driver Andrew Thomas has time to talk with Jonathan Mann and guard Nigel Adams while their colleagues fill the two locos with water from Dolgoch's historic wooden water tank.

Another view on 21 March 2016 as DOLGOCH takes water.

Just over one year later the grass is much greener as DOLGOCH waits to leave for Abergynolwyn on 31 March 2017.

Andrew Thomas is in charge again on 20 March 2018 as DOLGOCH takes water from the old Dolgoch water tank.

The scene is quite different on 6 July 2017 as TALYLLYN takes water while working the Victorian Train.

TALYLLYN has plenty of spectators as she takes water on 6 July 2017. They're not just the Victorian Train's passengers as a down train was due to arrive a few minutes later after crossing this train at Quarry Siding, just half a mile to the east.

The "platform" side of van no 5 with its sliding double doors and the booking office hatch in its ducket where tickets were sold for many years before the preservation era – and are still occasionally sold now! 6 July 2017.

Should I go up the valley to Nant Gwernol or down to Tywyn? Decisions, decisions! 9 August 2015.

...eman Ian Evans watches for the right-away with a down train at Dolgoch hauled by TALYLLYN on 9 August 2015.

There's a watering point at the down end of Dolgoch station as well as the historic wooden tank and a modern steel one a litt[le] to its east. All three draw water from a spring on the hillside a short distance above the station. EDWARD THOMAS takes wat[er] on 3 July 2018.

The tank is full and EDWARD THOMAS approaches Dolgoch viaduct on 3 July 2018.

SIR HAYDN sets off from Dolgoch with an up train on 13 April 2007, and crosses the cattle creep which allows access to th hillside from Dolgoch farm.

DOUGLAS heads away from Dolgoch through the woods on 12 March 2014.

TALYLLYN approaches Quarry Siding on 30 March 2017 during a brief sunny interval in what was otherwise a cloudy afternoon. Note her old saddle tank in the bank on the left. It was relocated here to provide shelter for people working on the line when the loco was provided with a new tank in the 1920s. I have only twice ever seen a steam ring like the one which the loco has just puffed out.

TALYLLYN brings empty wagons up the Fathew valley near Quarry Siding on 30th March 2017. Another footpath begins here which climbs high above the Dolgoch ravine and on to Mynydd Ty-Mawr, from where there are magnificent views over the valley right down to Tywyn.

DOLGOCH and TALYLLYN have left Quarry Siding and head up the valley near Tan-y-coed Uchaf on 31 March 2017.

DOLGOCH and TALYLLYN have passed Tan-y-coed Uchaf and approach Abergynolwyn on 31st March 2017. The entire valley between the Talyllyn pass and Bryncrug is glacial in origin. It follows the same fault line as Bala lake to the northeast, but a build-up of glacial moraine at this spot in prehistoric times led to the Afon Dysynni cutting through the hills to the north to find a new route to the sea. Another build-up of moraine further up the valley created Talyllyn lake. In place of the Dysynni the Afon Fathew rises hereabouts. It looks far too small for the valley until it reaches Dolgoch and joins the larger stream which flows through the Dolgoch ravine.

DOLGOCH stands with van no 5 at Abergynolwyn station on 9 July 2014.

DOLGOCH heads through the woods at Forestry Crossing, midway between Abergynolwyn and Nant Gwernol, on 9 July 2014.

DOLGOCH and a slate wagon pause at the site of the Abergynolwyn incline winding house on 21 March 2016. The incline was used to transport goods to the village and also to take away foul waste. Sadly the winding house disappeared in the early 1970s when the line beyond Abergynolwyn station, originally used only for slate traffic, was rebuilt to accommodate passenger trains. The drum is all that remains.

The carriage wheels squeal as TALYLLYN runs around the sharp curve just before Nant Gwernol station on 2 July 2017. The skip wagons are standing on a short section of the old mineral line which has been left in situ here, and its curve is even sharper!

Nant Gwernol station occupies the site of what were originally sidings at the foot of the Alltwydd cable incline, where wagons brought down from Bryn Eglwys slate quarry would be assembled into trains for onward transit to Tywyn. This scene, from one of Mr Williams's charters, was an attempt to replicate a photo from before Sir Haydn's time when a single passenger coach, hauled by TALYLLYN, was brought there to convey the quarry owners' family. DOLGOCH and TALYLLYN in the evening of 2 March 2016.

Another view of DOLGOCH and TALYLLYN at Nant Gwernol on 21 March 2016.

Journey's end! SIR HAYDN, now back in the preservation society's green paint scheme following overhaul at the Vale o Rheidol's works at Aberystwyth, stands at Nant Gwernol on 5 July 2019. She is seen from the footpath which follows the Alltwydd incline which began at what is now the railway's buffer stop. One feature which can't be seen from the platform is the enormous retaining wall, reaching far down the steeply sloping valley side, built back in the 1860's to support the old sidings.

SIR HAYDN runs round her train at Nant Gwernol on 5 July 2019. Though of course I didn't know it at the time this was to be my ~~final~~ Talyllyn photo before the onset of the Covid-19 pandemic. Let's hope it won't be too long before the railway reopens and we ~~can~~ all travel again.

The winding house and drum at the top of Alltwydd incline have been restored and are kept in good order. It marks the start of what was once the horse worked Galltymoelfre Tramroad, the route of which now forms an important part of the network of public footpaths created around Nant Gwernol when the extension from Abergynolwyn was built. There are striking views down to the Gwernol stream far below. For many years the remains of wrecked slate wagons could be seen around the stream. They were runaways from the Cantrybedd incline, the second of the three cable inclines needed for the railway to reach Bryn Eglwys, and have now been rescued for preservation. A much older footpath runs alongside the east bank of the stream. For some long forgotten reason it is known as the Shanghai Path and leads up the valley from Abergynolwyn. There are footbridges and the two paths make for excellent walks in between rides on the Talyllyn's trains. 22 March 2016.

In 2014 the coupling and connecting rods of TALYLLYN came adrift during a trip and suffered major damage. It was an especial tragedy since they formed some of the few original parts which had survived since the loco was built. Pendre works was fully committed to the overhaul of TOM ROLT but happily the Ffestiniog Railway's Boston Lodge works stepped in and carried out a comprehensive overhaul. Here TALYLLYN stands, with her leading and trailing wheelsets in the foreground, on 8 May 2014. The headboard refers to the sixtieth anniversary of the Ffestiniog Railway Society.

The loco's rear driving wheelsets are mounted on the wheel lathe at Boston Lodge and have been trued up. 8 May 2014.

he coupling and connecting rods and the motion are on the left in this photo on 8 May 2014. Beyond them are the downhill ower bogie of 0-4-4-0 Double Fairlie MERDDIN EMRYS, the first loco to have been built at Boston Lodge in 1879, and Lautoka ugar factory's 0-6-0 no 11, now named FIJI (Hudswell Clarke 972/1912). She had recently been restored to working order at e Statfold Barn Railway in Staffordshire and was visiting for running-in trips on the Welsh Highland Railway. The rest of ERDDIN EMRYS is just peeping into the left of the photo and on the right is part of 0-6-0 diesel hydraulic CASTELL RICCIETH, built at Boston Lodge in 1995 using parts produced by Baguley Drewry for a loco intended for Mozambique. They ere left on their hands when the order was cancelled.

The Talyllyn down under! 0-4-0T TYWYN is a 7¼ inch gauge loco, built in 1985 by Ray Bennett, a UK expat who spent man
years in Victoria before moving to Tununda in South Australia. Ray later sold her to Norm Wadeson, a towering figure in th
rescue of the 2ft 6ins gauge Puffing Billy Railway near Melbourne between 1953 and the 1970s. Nowadays the Puffing Billy lin
is by far the busiest and most successful heritage railway anywhere in the southern hemisphere, and one of the foremost touris
attractions in Victoria. It has for many years been twinned with the Talyllyn. The loco ran on the Kuralie Timber Tramway, Norm'
garden railway at his home in Baxter, Victoria, which reflected his knowledge of, and affection for, the state's narrow gaug
timber railways. The resemblance she bears to DOUGLAS is clear for all to see. I saw her at the Puffing Billy's workshops a
Belgrave on 25 July 2015. Victorian Railways' 2-6-0+0-6-2 Garratt no G42 (Beyer Peacock 6268/1926) stands on the right.

...he plates on the cab of TYWYN. The ...arter device with the Prince of Wales's ...eathers has been used since the ...reservation society's early days. It was ...ased on an old seal which Tom Rolt ...ound in the booking office at Wharf. ...YWYN was fitted with a new boiler ...fter 2010, but sadly Norm's health was ...eteriorating and the Puffing Billy's ...olunteers completed the loco's fitting ...ut work in 2015. By then Norm had ...noved into a nursing home but the ...olunteers were able to take the ...completed loco there for him to see, ...hortly before he died later that year. ...His family and friends still operate her at ...his old home.

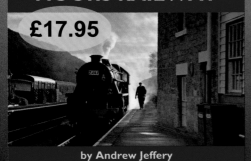